COMMERCIAL LAW
Essential Legal Terms Explained You Need To Know About Law on Commerce!

DR. PETER JOHNSON

Copyright © 2019

All rights reserved.

ISBN: 9781090656841

TEXT COPYRIGHT © [DR. PETER JOHNSON]

all rights reserved. No part of this guide may be reproduced in any form without permission in writing from the publisher except in the case of brief quotations embodied in critical articles or reviews.

Legal & disclaimer

The information contained in this book and its contents is not designed to replace or take the place of any form of medical or professional advice; and is not meant to replace the need for independent medical, financial, legal or other professional advice or services, as may be required. The content and information in this book have been provided for educational and entertainment purposes only.

The content and information contained in this book have been compiled from sources deemed reliable, and it is accurate to the best of the author's knowledge, information, and belief. However, the author cannot guarantee its accuracy and validity and cannot be held liable for any errors and/or omissions. Further, changes are periodically made to this book as and when needed. Where appropriate and/or necessary, you must consult a professional (including but not limited to your doctor, attorney, financial advisor or such other professional advisor) before using any of the suggested remedies, techniques, or information in this book.

Upon using the contents and information contained in this book, you agree to hold harmless the author from and against any damages, costs, and expenses, including any legal fees potentially resulting from the application of any of the information provided by this book. This disclaimer applies to any loss, damages or injury caused by the use and application, whether directly or indirectly, of any advice or information presented, whether for breach of contract, tort, negligence, personal injury, criminal intent, or under any other cause of action.

You agree to accept all risks of using the information presented inside this book.

You agree that by continuing to read this book, where appropriate and/or necessary, you shall consult a professional (including but not limited to your doctor, attorney, or financial advisor or such other advisor as needed) before using any of the suggested remedies, techniques, or information in this book.

Table of Contents

Introduction 16

Interpretation Of Terms 17

Traders 20

Obligation Of Traders To Register Business 21

Commercial Associations 22

Principle Of Traders' Equality Before Law In Commercial Activities 23

Principle Of Traders' Equality Before Law In Commercial Activities 24

Principle Of Freedom And Freewill To Agreement In Commercial Activities 25

Principle Of Application Of Customs In Commercial Activities Pre-Established Between Parties 26

Principle Of Application Of Practices In Commercial Activities 27

Principle Of Protection Of Legitimate Interests Of Consumers 28

Principle Of Recognition Of Legal Validity Of Data Messages In Commercial Activities 29

Form Of Contracts For Purchase And Sale Of Goods 30

Application Of Urgent Measures With Respect To Domestically Circulated Goods 31

International Purchase And Sale Of Goods 32

Labels For Domestically Circulated, Exported And Imported Goods 33

Delivery Of Goods And Goods-Related Documents 34

Place Of Delivery Of Goods 35

Responsibilities Upon Delivery Of Goods Where Carriers Are Involved 36

Time Limit For Delivery Of Goods 37

Delivery Of Goods Before The Agreed Time 38

Goods Which Are Not Appropriate To Contracts 39

Liability For Goods Which Are Not Appropriate To Contracts 40

Remedies In Case Of Delivery Of Goods In Insufficient Quantity Or Delivery Of Goods Not Appropriate To Contracts 41

Delivery Of Goods-Related Documents 42

Delivery Of Goods In Excessive Quantity 43

Pre-Delivery Examination Of Goods 44

Obligation To Assure The Ownership Right Over Goods 45

Obligation To Assure Intellectual Property Rights Over Goods 46

Obligation Of The Seller In Cases Where Goods Are Subject To Measures Of Security For Performance Of Civil Obligations .. 47

Obligation To Provide Warranty For Goods 48

Payment 49

Suspension Of Payment For Goods 50

Determination Of Prices 51

Pricing By Weight 52

Place Of Payment 53

Time Limit For Payment 54

Receipt Of Goods 55

Pass Of Risks In Cases Where There Is A Fixed Place Of Delivery Of Goods 56

Pass Of Risks In Cases Where There Is No Fixed Place Of Delivery Of Goods 57

Pass Of Risks In Cases Where Goods Are Handed Over To A Bailee That Is Not A Carrier 58

Pass Of Risks In Case Of Purchase And Sale Of Goods In Transportation 59

Pass Of Risks In Other Cases 60

Time Of Transferring Ownership Of Goods 61

Purchase And Sale Of Goods Though The Goods Exchange .. 62

Contracts For Purchase And Sale Of Goods Through The Goods Exchange 63

Rights And Obligations Of Parties To Forward Contracts 64

Rights And Obligations Of Parties To Option Contracts 65

The Goods Exchange 66

Prohibited Acts In Activities Of Purchase And Sale Of Goods Through The Goods Exchange 67

Forms Of Service Contracts 68

Obligations Of The Service Providers 69

Obligations Of The Service Providers According To Performance Result 70

Obligations Of The Service Providers To Make The Best Effort 71

Cooperation Among Service Providers 72

Time Limit For Completion Of Services 73

Customers' Requests For Changes During The Provision Of Services 74

Continued Provision Of Services After The Expiration Of The Time Limit For Completing The Provision Of Services 75

Obligations Of Customers 76

Service Charge Rate 77

Time Limit For Payment 78

Sale Promotion 79

Provision Of Sale Promotion Service 80

Sale Promotion Service Contracts 81

Forms Of Sale Promotion 82

Sale Promotion Goods And Services 83

Goods And Services Used For Sale Promotion, Sale Promotion Discount Rates 84

Rights Of Traders Conducting Sale Promotion 85

Keeping Secret Information On Sale Promotion Programs And Details 86

Prohibited Acts In Sale Promotion Activities 87

Registration For Sale Promotion Activities With, And Notification Of Sale Promotion Results To, The State Management Agency In Charge Of Commerce 88

Commercial Advertising 89

Provision Of Commercial Advertising Services 90

Commercial Advertising Products 91

Means Of Commercial Advertising 92

Use Of Means Of Commercial Advertising 93

Protection Of Intellectual Property Rights Over Commercial Advertising Products 94

Prohibited Commercial Advertisements 95

Commercial Advertising Service Contracts 96

Rights Of Commercial Advertising Hirers 97

Obligations Of Commercial Advertising Hirers 98

Rights Of Commercial Advertising Service Providers 99

Obligations Of Commercial Advertising Service Providers....100

Commercial Advertising Distributors 101

Obligations Of Commercial Advertising Distributors 102

Display And Introduction Of Goods And Services....................103

Provision Of Goods/Service Display And Introduction Services 104

Forms Of Display And Introduction Of Goods And Services 105

Conditions For Displayed And Introduced Goods And/Or Services 106

Cases Where Display And Introduction Of Goods And/Or Services Are Prohibited...107

Contracts For Provision Of Goods And/Or Service Display And Introduction Services 108

Rights Of Goods And/Or Service Display And Introduction Service Hirers 109

Obligations Of Goods And/Or Service Display And Introduction Service Hirers 110

Rights Of Goods And/Or Service Display And Introduction Service Providers 111

Obligations Of Goods And/Or Service Display And Introduction Service Providers..112

Trade Fairs And Exhibitions...113

Provision Of Trade Fair And Exhibition Services....................114

Organization Of And Participation In Overseas Trade Fairs And Exhibitions 115

Goods And/Or Services Participating In Overseas Trade Fairs And Exhibitions 116

Rights And Obligations Of Organizations And Individuals Participating In Trade Fairs And Exhibitions 117

Rights And Obligations Of Traders Organizing Or Participating In Overseas Trade Fairs And Exhibitions 118

Rights And Obligations Of Traders Providing Trade Fair And Exhibition Services 119

Agreement On Representation For Traders 120

Scope Of Representation 121

Duration Of Representation For Traders 122

Obligations Of The Representative 123

Obligations Of The Principal 124

Payment For Any Expense Incurred 125

Lien 126

Commercial Brokerage 127

Obligations Of Commercial Brokers 128

Obligations Of Principals 129

The Right To Enjoy Brokerage Remuneration 130

Payment Of Expenses Incurred In Relation To Brokerage ... 131

Purchase And Sale Of Goods By Mandated Dealers 132

Mandatories 133

Mandators 134

Mandated Goods 135

Mandate Contracts 136

Sub-Mandate To A Third Party 137

Multilateral Mandate 138

Rights Of Mandators 139

Obligations Of Mandators 140

Rights Of Mandatories 141

Obligations Of Mandatories 142

Commercial Agency 143

Principals And Agents 144

Agency Contracts 145

Forms Of Agency 146

Ownership Right In Commercial Agency 147

Agency Remuneration 148

Rights Of Principals 149

Obligations Of Principals 150

Rights Of Agents 151

Obligations Of Agents 152

Payment In Agency Activities 153

Logistic Services 154

Conditions For Logistic Service Provision............................... 155

Rights And Obligations Of Traders Providing Logistic Services
 156

Rights And Obligations Of Customers 157

Liability Exemption For Traders Providing Logistic Services
 158

Limitation To Liability 159

The Right To Withhold And Dispose Of Goods 160

Obligations Of Traders Providing Logistic Services When
Withholding Goods.. 161

Transit Of Goods 162

Right To Transit Goods 163

Prohibited Acts During Transit 164

Goods Transit Services 165

Transit Service Contracts 166

Rights And Obligations Of Transit Service Hirers 167

Assessment Services 168

Contents Of Assessment 169

Traders Providing Commercial Assessment Services 170

Criteria Of Assessors 171

Assessment Certificates 172

Legal Validity Of Assessment Certificates With Respect To Assessment Requesters 173

Rights And Obligations Of Traders Providing Assessment Services 174

Rights Of Customers 175

Obligations Of Customers 176

Fines And Damages In Case Of Incorrect Assessment Results 177

Assessment At The Request Of State Agencies 178

Lease Of Goods 179

Rights And Obligations Of Lessors 180

Rights And Obligations Of Lessees 181

Repair Or Alteration Of Original Status Of Leased Goods 182

Liability For Loss Occurring In The Lease Duration 183

Pass Of Risks Incurred To Leased Goods 184

Leased Goods Inappropriate To Contracts 185

Rejection Of Goods 186

Rectification Or Replacement Of Leased Goods Inappropriate To Contracts 187

Acceptance Of Leased Goods 188

Withdrawal Of Acceptance 189

Sub-Lease 190

Benefits Arising In The Lease Duration 191

Change Of Ownership In The Lease Duration 192

Commercial Franchise 193

Commercial Franchise Contracts 194

Rights Of Franchisors 195

Obligations Of Franchisors 196

Rights Of Franchisees 197

Obligations Of Franchisees 198

Types Of Commercial Remedies 199

Application Of Commercial Remedies Against Insubstantial Breaches 200

Cases Of Exemption From Liability For Breaching Acts 201

Notification And Certification Of Cases Of Liability Exemption 202

Extension Of Time Limit For Performance Of Contracts, Or Refusal To Perform Contracts In Force Majeure Circumstances 203

Specific Performance Of Contracts 204

Fine Level 205

Damages 206

Grounds For Liability To Pay Damages 207

Burden Of Proof Of Loss 208

Obligations To Mitigate Loss 209

Right To Claim Interest On Delayed Payment 210

Relationship Between Remedy Of Fines And Remedy Of
Damages 211

Suspension Of Performance Of Contracts 212

Legal Consequences Of Suspension Of Performance Of
Contracts 213

Stoppage Of Performance Of Contracts 214

Legal Consequences Of Stoppage Of Performance Of Contracts
.... 215

Cancellation Of Contracts 216

Cancellation Of Contracts In Case Of Delivery Of Goods Or
Provision Of Services In Installments 217

Legal Consequences Of Cancellation Of Contracts 218

Notification Of Suspension Of Performance Of Contracts,
Stoppage Of Performance Of Contracts Or Cancellation Of
Contracts 219

Right To Claim Damages When Other Remedies Have Been
Applied 220

Forms Of Resolution Of Disputes 221

Acts Of Violation Of Commercial Law 222

Forms Of Handling Of Violations Of Commercial Law 223

Sanctioning Of Administrative Violations In Commercial Activities 224

Conclusion 225

Check Out Other Books 226

INTRODUCTION

Thank you and congratulate you for downloading the book *"COMMERCIAL LAW: Essential Legal Terms Explained You Need To Know About Law on Commerce!"*

With a clear, concise, and engaging writing style, Dr. Peter Johnson will help you with a practical understanding of commercial law topics *about international purchase and sale of goods, delivery of goods, place of delivery of goods, time limit for delivery of goods, obligation to provide warranty for goods, payment, suspension of payment for goods, time limit for payment, receipt of goods, the goods exchange, service contracts, sale promotion, commercial advertising, trade fairs and exhibitions, commercial brokerage, mandatories, mandators, mandated goods, mandate contracts, logistic services, transit of goods, commercial franchise, cancellation of contracts and* **much much more**. This book delivers extensive coverage of every aspect of the law and details the duties a paralegal is expected to perform when working within law on commerce. High-level, comprehensive coverage is combined with cutting-edge developments and foundational concepts.

As the author of the book, I promise this book will be an invaluable source of legal reference for professionals, international lawyers, law students, business professionals and anyone else who want to improve their use of legal terminology, succinct clarification of legal terms and have a better understanding of law on lawyers. All legal terms and phrases are well written and explained clearly in plain English.

Thank you again for purchasing this book, and I hope you enjoy it.

Let's get started!

INTERPRETATION OF TERMS

1. *Commercial activities* mean activities for the purpose of generating profits, including: sale and purchase of goods, provision of services, investment, commercial promotion and other activities for the profit purpose.

2. *Goods* include:

a/ All types of movables, including those to be formed in the future;

b/ Things attached to land;

3. *Custom in commercial activities* means a code of conduct that has an explicit meaning, is established and repeated time and again for a long period of time between and implicitly recognized by involved parties in order identify their respective rights and obligations in commercial contracts.

4. *Commercial practice* means a custom that is widely recognized in commercial activities in an area, a region or a commercial domain, has an explicit meaning, and is recognized by involved parties in order to identify their respective rights and obligations in commercial activities.

5. *Data message* means information created, sent, received and stored in electronic media.

6. *Purchase and sale of goods* mean commercial activities whereby the seller is obliged to deliver goods, transfer ownership of goods to the purchaser and receive payment; the purchaser is obliged to pay to the seller and receive goods and the ownership thereof as agreed.

7. *Provision of services* means commercial activities whereby a party (hereinafter referred to as the service provider) is obliged to provide a service to another party and receive payment; the service-using party (hereinafter referred to as the customer) is obliged to pay to the service provider and use the service as agreed.

8. *Commercial services* shall include services associated with the purchase and sale of goods;

9. *Commercial promotion* means activities of promoting and seeking opportunities for the purchase or sale of goods and provision of services, including sale promotion, commercial advertisement, display and exhibition of goods and services, and trade fairs and exhibitions.

10. *Commercial intermediary activities* mean activities carried out by a trader to effect commercial transactions for one or several identified traders, including representation for traders, commercial brokerage, goods sale or purchase entrustment, and commercial agency.

11. *Commercial assets* are all assets under the lawful ownership or use right of a trader to serve commercial activities such as offices, shops, warehouses, equipment, goods, trade names, signboards, trademarks, goods distribution and services provision networks.

12. *Contractual breach* means the failure of a party to perform, to fully or properly perform its obligations according to the agreement between the involved parties or the provisions of Commercial law.

13. *Substantial breach* means a contractual breach by a party, which causes damage to the other party to an extent that the other party cannot achieve the purpose of the entry into the contract.

14. *Origin of goods* means a country or a territory where all the goods are turned out or where the last stage of substantial processing of goods is performed in cases where many countries or territories join in the process of producing such goods.

15. *Forms of validity equivalent to documents* include telegraph, telex, facsimile, data message and other forms provided for by law.

TRADERS

1. Traders include lawfully established economic organizations and individuals that conduct commercial activities in an independent and regular manner and have business registrations.

2. Traders are entitled to conduct commercial activities in occupations and sectors, in geographical areas, in forms and by modes which are not banned by law.

3. The right of traders to conduct lawful commercial activities is protected by the State.

4. The State exercises for a definite time its monopoly over commercial activities in respect to a number of goods and services or in a number of geographical areas in order to ensure the national interests. The Government shall specify the lists of goods, services and geographical areas subject to the State monopoly.

OBLIGATION OF TRADERS TO REGISTER BUSINESS

Traders are obliged to register their business according to the provisions of law. Where traders have not yet registered their business, they are still held responsible for all of their activities according to the provisions of Commercial law and other provisions of law.

COMMERCIAL ASSOCIATIONS

1. Commercial associations are established to protect the legitimate rights and interests of traders, mobilize traders to take part in commercial development, and disseminate and propagate the provisions of law on commerce.

2. Commercial associations are organized and operate according to the provisions of law on associations.

PRINCIPLE OF TRADERS' EQUALITY BEFORE LAW IN COMMERCIAL ACTIVITIES

Traders of all economic sectors are equal before law in commercial activities.

PRINCIPLE OF TRADERS' EQUALITY BEFORE LAW IN COMMERCIAL ACTIVITIES

Traders of all economic sectors are equal before law in commercial activities.

PRINCIPLE OF FREEDOM AND FREEWILL TO AGREEMENT IN COMMERCIAL ACTIVITIES

1. Parties have the rights of freedom to reach agreements not in contravention of the provisions of law, fine traditions and customs and social ethics in order to establish their rights and obligations in commercial activities. The State respects and protects such rights.

2. In commercial activities, the parties shall act on their own freewill, and neither party is allowed to impose its own will on, to force, intimidate or obstruct, the other party.

PRINCIPLE OF APPLICATION OF CUSTOMS IN COMMERCIAL ACTIVITIES PRE-ESTABLISHED BETWEEN PARTIES

Except otherwise agreed, the parties shall be regarded as automatically applying customs in commercial activities pre-established between them which they have already known or ought to know, provided that such customs are not contrary to the provisions of law.

PRINCIPLE OF APPLICATION OF PRACTICES IN COMMERCIAL ACTIVITIES

Where it is neither provided for by law nor agreed by the parties, and there exist no customs pre-established between them, commercial practices shall be applied provided that such practices are not contrary to the principles provided for in commercial law and the Civil Code.

PRINCIPLE OF PROTECTION OF LEGITIMATE INTERESTS OF CONSUMERS

1. Traders conducting commercial activities are obliged to provide consumers with sufficient and truthful information on goods and/or services they trade in or provide and take responsibility for the accuracy of such information.

2. Traders conducting commercial activities must be responsible for the quality and lawfulness of goods and/or services they trade in or provide.

PRINCIPLE OF RECOGNITION OF LEGAL VALIDITY OF DATA MESSAGES IN COMMERCIAL ACTIVITIES

In commercial activities, data messages which satisfy all technical conditions and standards provided for by law shall be recognized legally valid as documents.

FORM OF CONTRACTS FOR PURCHASE AND SALE OF GOODS

1. Contracts for sale and purchase of goods may be expressed in verbal or written form or established by specific acts.

2. For types of contracts for purchase and sale of goods, which, as provided for by law, must be made in writing, such provisions must be complied with.

APPLICATION OF URGENT MEASURES WITH RESPECT TO DOMESTICALLY CIRCULATED GOODS

1. Goods legally and domestically circulated may be subject to the application of one or all of such measures as compulsory withdrawal from circulation, circulation ban, circulation suspension, conditional circulation, or compulsory circulation permission in the following cases:

a/ Where such goods constitute sources or transmitters of various epidemics and diseases;

b/ Where an emergency circumstance occurs.

2. Specific conditions, order, procedures and competence for announcing the application of urgent measures to domestically circulated goods shall comply with the provisions of law.

INTERNATIONAL PURCHASE AND SALE OF GOODS

1. International purchase and sale of goods shall be conducted in form of export, import, temporary import for re-export, temporary export for re-import and transfer through border-gates.

2. International purchase and sale of goods shall be conducted on the basis of written contracts or other forms of equal legal validity.

LABELS FOR DOMESTICALLY CIRCULATED, EXPORTED AND IMPORTED GOODS

1. Goods labels mean writings, prints, drawings or photos of texts, pictures or images, which are stuck, printed, affixed, molded, carved or engraved directly on goods or their commercial packing or other materials which are attached to the goods or their packing.

2. All goods that are domestically circulated, imported and exported must have their labels, except for some cases specified by law.

3. Contents which must be inscribed in goods labels and the labeling of goods shall comply with regulations of the Government.

DELIVERY OF GOODS AND GOODS-RELATED DOCUMENTS

1. The seller must deliver goods and relevant documents, as agreed in contracts on quantity, quality, packing and preservation modes and other contractual terms.

2. In cases where there is no specific agreement, the seller is obliged to deliver goods and relevant documents according to the provisions of commercial law.

PLACE OF DELIVERY OF GOODS

1. The seller is obliged to deliver goods at the agreed place.

2. In cases where there is no agreement on place of goods delivery, such a place shall be specified as follows:

a/ In cases where goods are things attached to land, the seller must deliver goods at the place where such goods exist;

b/ In cases where the contract contains a provision on goods transportation, the seller is obliged to deliver goods to the first carrier;

c/ In cases where the contract contains no provision on goods transportation, and at the time the contract is entered into, the parties know the location of the goods storage, the place of goods loading or the place of goods manufacture, the seller shall have to deliver the goods at such place;

d/ In other cases, the seller shall have to deliver goods at his/her place of business, or his/her place of residence identified at the time the purchase and sale contract is entered into in cases he/she has no place of business.

RESPONSIBILITIES UPON DELIVERY OF GOODS WHERE CARRIERS ARE INVOLVED

1. Where goods are handed over to the carrier without being identified with specific signs or marks on them, accompanied with transportation documents or otherwise, the seller must notify the purchaser of the handover of goods to the carrier and clearly identify names and method of recognizing transported goods.

2. Where the seller is obliged to arrange the goods transportation, the seller shall have to enter into necessary contracts for the transportation of goods to the destination by means of transportation suitable to specific circumstances and under normal conditions for such modes of transportation.

3. Where the seller is not obliged to purchase insurance for the goods in the course of transportation and if requested by the purchaser, the seller must supply to the purchaser all necessary information on the goods and the transportation thereof to enable the purchaser to purchase insurance for the goods.

TIME LIMIT FOR DELIVERY OF GOODS

1. The seller must deliver goods at the time already agreed upon in the contract;

2. Where only the time limit for delivery of goods is agreed upon without a specific time for delivery of goods, the seller may deliver goods at any time within such time limit and must notify the purchaser of the delivery in advance;

3. Where there is no agreement on the time limit for delivery of goods, the seller must deliver goods within a reasonable time limit after the contract is entered into.

DELIVERY OF GOODS BEFORE THE AGREED TIME

Where the seller delivers goods earlier than the agreed time, the purchaser may receive or reject the goods, unless otherwise agreed upon by the parties.

GOODS WHICH ARE NOT APPROPRIATE TO CONTRACTS

1. Where it is not specified in the contract, goods shall be considered not appropriate to the contract when they fall into one of the following cases:

a/ They are not suitable to common use purposes of goods of the same type;

b/ They are not suitable to any specific purpose that has been notified by the purchaser to the seller or the seller should have known at the time the contract is entered into;

c/ Their quality is not the same as the quality of the samples previously handed over by the seller to the purchaser;

d/ They are not preserved or packaged by a method common to such goods, or not preserved by proper preserving methods in cases where no common preserving method is available.

2. The purchaser may reject the goods if such goods are not appropriate to the contract.

LIABILITY FOR GOODS WHICH ARE NOT APPROPRIATE TO CONTRACTS

Unless otherwise agreed upon by the parties, the liability for goods which are not appropriate to contracts is provided for as follows:

1. The seller shall not be liable for any defect of the goods if the purchaser, at the time the contract is entered into, knew or should have known such defect;

2. The seller shall be liable for any defect of the goods which already exists before the time of passing the risk to the purchaser despite the fact that such defect may be discovered after passing the risks.

3. The seller shall be liable for defects of goods occurring after the pass of risks if such defects are attributable to contract breaches by the seller.

REMEDIES IN CASE OF DELIVERY OF GOODS IN INSUFFICIENT QUANTITY OR DELIVERY OF GOODS NOT APPROPRIATE TO CONTRACTS

1. Unless otherwise agreed, and where the contract only provides for a time limit for delivery of goods and does not determine a specific time for delivery of goods, and the seller delivers goods before the expiration of such time limit but in insufficient quantity or goods not appropriate to the contract, the seller may still deliver the deficit quantity of goods or provide substitute goods which are appropriate to the contract or remedy the inappropriateness of the goods within the remaining duration.

2. When the seller causes disadvantages or unreasonable costs to the purchaser, the purchaser shall have the right to request the seller to deal with such disadvantages or bear such costs.

DELIVERY OF GOODS-RELATED DOCUMENTS

1. Where there is an agreement on the delivery of documents, the seller is obliged to deliver all goods-related documents to the purchaser within the time limit, at the place and by mode already agreed.

2. Where there is no agreement on the time limit and place for delivery of goods-related documents to the purchaser, the seller must deliver such documents to the purchaser within a reasonable time limit and at a convenient place so that the purchaser can receive the goods.

3. Where the seller has delivered goods-related documents before the agreed time, the seller can still rectify errors of such documents within the remaining duration of the time limit.

4. When the seller causes disadvantages or unreasonable costs to the purchaser, the purchaser shall have the right to request the seller to deal with such disadvantages or bear such costs.

DELIVERY OF GOODS IN EXCESSIVE QUANTITY

1. Where the seller delivers goods in excessive quantity, the purchaser may reject or accept such excessive quantity of goods.

2. Where the purchaser accepts the excessive quantity of goods, the purchaser must pay for that quantity at the price agreed in the contract unless otherwise agreed upon by the parties.

PRE-DELIVERY EXAMINATION OF GOODS

1. Where it is agreed by the parties that the purchaser or the purchaser's representative shall examine the goods before the delivery, the seller must ensure that the purchaser or the purchaser's representative shall be given conditions for conducting such examination.

2. Except where it is otherwise agreed, the purchaser or the purchaser's representative must examine the goods within the shortest period of time allowed by practical circumstances. Where the contract provides for the transportation of goods, the examination of goods may be postponed until the goods are transported to the destination.

3. Where the purchaser or the purchaser's representative does not conduct the examination of goods before the delivery of goods as agreed, the seller may deliver the goods according to the contract.

4. The seller shall not be liable for defects of goods which the purchaser or the purchaser's representative has known or should have known but failed to notify them to the seller within a reasonable time limit after the examination of goods.

5. The seller shall be liable for defects of goods already examined by the purchaser or the purchaser's representative if the defects of the goods cannot be detected in the course of examination through common measures and the seller knew or should have known such defects but failed to notify them to the purchaser.

OBLIGATION TO ASSURE THE OWNERSHIP RIGHT OVER GOODS

The seller must assure that:

1. The ownership right of the purchaser over goods sold is not disputed by any third party;

2. The goods are lawful;

3. The handover of the goods is lawful.

OBLIGATION TO ASSURE INTELLECTUAL PROPERTY RIGHTS OVER GOODS

1. The seller must not sell goods infringing upon intellectual property rights. The seller shall be held responsible for any dispute related intellectual property rights over goods sold.

2. Where the purchaser requests the seller to observe technical drawings, designs, formulas or specifications furnished by the purchaser, the purchaser shall be liable for complaints related to infringements of intellectual property rights which arise from the fact that the seller has complied with the request of the purchaser.

OBLIGATION OF THE SELLER IN CASES WHERE GOODS ARE SUBJECT TO MEASURES OF SECURITY FOR PERFORMANCE OF CIVIL OBLIGATIONS

Where the goods sold are subject to measures of security for performance of civil obligations, the seller must notify the purchaser of such security measures and must obtain the consent of the security beneficiary regarding the sale of such goods.

OBLIGATION TO PROVIDE WARRANTY FOR GOODS

1. Where goods are purchased and sold under warranty, the seller shall have to provide warranty for such goods according to the agreed contents and duration.

2. The seller must fulfill the warranty obligation as soon as the practical situation permits.

3. The seller must bear all warranty expenses unless otherwise agreed.

PAYMENT

1. The purchaser is obliged to pay for goods and receive goods as agreed upon.

2. The purchaser must comply with the payment modes and make the payment according to the agreed order and procedures and the provisions of law.

3. The purchaser shall still have to pay for goods in cases where goods are lost or damaged after the time the risk is passed from the seller to the purchaser, except for cases where the loss or damage is caused due to the fault of the seller.

SUSPENSION OF PAYMENT FOR GOODS

Unless otherwise agreed, the suspension of payment for goods is provided for as follows:

1. The purchaser that has proofs of deceit of the seller shall have the right to suspend the payment.

2. The purchaser that has proofs that the goods are subject to a dispute shall have the right to suspend the payment until the said dispute is settled.

3. The purchaser that has proofs that the seller has delivered goods which do not conform with the contract shall have the right to suspend the payment until the seller remedy such inconformity.

DETERMINATION OF PRICES

Where there is neither agreement on goods price or on the price-determining method nor other price indexes, the goods price shall be determined according to the price of such type of goods under similar conditions on mode of goods delivery, time of goods purchase and sale, geographical market, payment mode and other conditions which affect the prices.

PRICING BY WEIGHT

Unless otherwise agreed, if the goods price is determined according to the weight of the goods, such weight must be net weight.

PLACE OF PAYMENT

Where there is no agreement on specific place of payment, the purchaser must pay to the seller at one of the following places:

1. The seller's place of business, which is identified at the time of entering into the contract; or the seller's place of residence where the seller has no place of business.

2. The place where the goods or documents are delivered, if the payment is made concurrently with the delivery of goods or documents.

TIME LIMIT FOR PAYMENT

Unless otherwise agreed, the time limit for payment is provided for as follows:

1. The purchaser must make payment to the seller at the time the seller delivers the goods or the goods-related documents.

2. The purchaser is not obliged to make payment until the goods examination can be completed.

RECEIPT OF GOODS

The purchaser is obliged to receive the goods as agreed upon and do appropriate things to help the seller deliver the goods.

PASS OF RISKS IN CASES WHERE THERE IS A FIXED PLACE OF DELIVERY OF GOODS

Unless otherwise agreed, if the seller is obliged to deliver the goods to the purchaser at a particular place, the risk of goods loss or damage shall be passed to the purchaser as soon as the goods are delivered to the purchaser or the person authorized by the purchaser to receive the goods at such place, even in cases where the seller is authorized to retain the documents which establish the ownership rights over the goods.

PASS OF RISKS IN CASES WHERE THERE IS NO FIXED PLACE OF DELIVERY OF GOODS

Unless otherwise agreed, if the contract contains provisions on the goods transportation and the seller is not obliged to deliver the goods at a given place, the risk of goods loss or damage shall be passed to the purchaser as soon as the goods are delivered to the first carrier.

PASS OF RISKS IN CASES WHERE GOODS ARE HANDED OVER TO A BAILEE THAT IS NOT A CARRIER

Unless otherwise agreed, if the goods are being kept by a bailee that is not a carrier, the risks of goods loss or damage shall be passed to the purchaser in one of the following cases:

1. Upon receipt by the purchaser of documents of title to the goods;

2. Upon the confirmation by the bailee of the purchaser's right to possession of the goods.

PASS OF RISKS IN CASE OF PURCHASE AND SALE OF GOODS IN TRANSPORTATION

Unless otherwise agreed, if the subject matter of the contract is goods in transportation, the risk of goods loss or damage shall be passed to the purchaser as from the time the contract is entered into.

PASS OF RISKS IN OTHER CASES

Unless otherwise agreed, the pass of risks in other cases is provided for as follows:

1. The risk of goods loss or damage is to be passed to the purchaser as from the time the goods fall under the purchaser's right of disposal and the purchaser breaches the contract by rejecting the goods.

2. **Risk** of goods loss or damage is not to be passed to the purchaser if the goods are neither clearly identified by their signs, codes or bills of transportation, nor notified to the purchaser, nor identified by any means.

TIME OF TRANSFERRING OWNERSHIP OF GOODS

Unless otherwise provided for by law or agreed upon by the parties, ownership of goods shall be passed from the seller to the purchaser as from the time of handover of the goods.

PURCHASE AND SALE OF GOODS THOUGH THE GOODS EXCHANGE

1. Purchase and sale of goods through the Goods Exchange mean commercial activities whereby the parties agree to purchase and sell a defined quantity of goods of a defined type through the Goods Exchange under the standards of the Goods Exchange, at a price agreed upon at the time the contract is entered into, and with the time of goods delivery determined to be a specific point of time in the future.

2. The Government shall specify activities of purchase and sale of goods through the Goods Exchange.

CONTRACTS FOR PURCHASE AND SALE OF GOODS THROUGH THE GOODS EXCHANGE

1. Contracts for purchase and sale of goods through the Goods Exchange include forward contracts and option contracts.

2. Forward contract means an agreement whereby the seller undertakes to deliver and the purchaser undertakes to receive the goods at a specific point of time in the future under the contract.

3. Call option or put option contract means an agreement whereby the purchaser has the right to purchase or sell a specific goods at a pre-fixed price level (hereinafter called executed price) and must pay a certain sum of money to buy this right (hereinafter called option money). The option purchaser may opt to effect or not to effect such purchase or sale of goods.

RIGHTS AND OBLIGATIONS OF PARTIES TO FORWARD CONTRACTS

1. Where the seller delivers the goods under the contract, the purchaser is obliged to receive the goods and pay for them.

2. Where the parties agree that the purchaser may make cash payment and reject the goods, the purchaser shall have to pay to the seller a sum of money equal to the difference between the price agreed upon in the contract and the market price announced by the Goods Exchange at the time the contract is performed.

3. Where the parties agree that the purchaser may make cash payment and refuse to deliver the goods, the seller shall have to pay to the purchaser a sum of money equal to the difference between the market price announced by the Goods Exchange at the time the contract is performed and the price agreed upon in the contract.

RIGHTS AND OBLIGATIONS OF PARTIES TO OPTION CONTRACTS

1. The call option or put option purchaser shall have to pay for option purchase in order to become call option or put option holder. The sum of money to be paid for option purchase shall be agreed upon by the parties.

2. The call option holder has the right to purchase but is not obliged to purchase goods ascertained in the contract. Where the call option holder decides to perform the contract, the seller shall be obliged to sell goods to the call option holder. The seller that has no goods to deliver shall have to pay to the call option holder a sum of money equal to the difference between the price agreed upon in the contract and the market price announced by the Goods Exchange at the time the contract is performed.

3. The put option holder has the right to sell but is not obliged to sell goods ascertained in the contract. Where the put option holder decides to perform the contract, the purchaser shall be obliged to purchase goods from the put option holder. Where the purchaser does not purchase goods, it shall have to pay to the put option holder a sum of money equal to the difference between the market price announced by the Goods Exchange at the time the contract is performed and the price agreed upon in the contract.

4. Where the call option or put option holder decides not to perform the contract within the valid duration of the contract, the contract shall automatically be invalidated.

THE GOODS EXCHANGE

1. The Goods Exchange has the following functions:

a/ Providing the material - technical conditions necessary for transactions of purchasing or selling goods;

b/ Running trading operations;

c/ Listing specific prices formed at the Goods Exchange at each specific time.

2. The Government shall specify the conditions for the establishment of the Goods Exchange, the powers and tasks of the Goods Exchange, and the approval of the operation charter of the Goods Exchange.

PROHIBITED ACTS IN ACTIVITIES OF PURCHASE AND SALE OF GOODS THROUGH THE GOODS EXCHANGE

1. Staff members of the Goods Exchange shall not be allowed to conduct the brokerage for, purchase or sale of goods through the Goods Exchange.

2. Parties involved in the purchase and sale of goods through the Goods Exchange must not conduct the following acts:

a/ Committing fraudulences or deceits about volumes of goods in forward or option contracts which are transacted or may be transacted, and fraudulences and deceits about real prices of goods in forward or option contracts;

b/ Supplying false information on transactions, the market or prices of goods purchased or sold through the Goods Exchange;

c/ Applying illegal measures to cause disorder of the goods market at the Goods Exchange;

d/ Committing other prohibited acts provided for by law.

FORMS OF SERVICE CONTRACTS

1. A service contract shall be expressed in verbal or written form or established with specific acts.

2. For those types of service contract which are required by law to be made in writing, such requirement must be abided by.

OBLIGATIONS OF THE SERVICE PROVIDERS

Unless otherwise agreed, the service provider shall have the following obligations:

1. To provide services and fully perform related jobs in accordance with agreements and the provisions of commercial law;

2. To preserve and hand back to their customers documents and means supplied to them for the service provision after the completion thereof;

3. To promptly notify to their customers in cases where information and documents are insufficient and means are inadequate for completion of the service provision;

4. To keep secret information they know in the course of service provision if so agreed upon by the parties or provided for by law.

OBLIGATIONS OF THE SERVICE PROVIDERS ACCORDING TO PERFORMANCE RESULT

Unless otherwise agreed, if the nature of the type of service to be provided requires a service provider to achieve a certain result, the service provider must conduct the service provision with a result appropriate with the terms and purpose of the contract. Where the contract does not specify the standards of result to be achieved, the service provider must conduct the service provision with a result compliant with the common standards applicable to such type of service.

OBLIGATIONS OF THE SERVICE PROVIDERS TO MAKE THE BEST EFFORT

Unless otherwise agreed, if the nature of the type of service to be provided requires a service provider to make the best effort to achieve a desired result, the service provider shall perform the obligation of service provision with the best effort and the highest capacity.

COOPERATION AMONG SERVICE PROVIDERS

Where under a contractual agreement or on the basis of practical circumstances, a service is jointly performed by many service providers or performed by a service provider in cooperation with other service providers, each of the said service providers shall have the following obligations:

1. To exchange and communicate to each other information on the performance progress and its demands related to the service provision, at the same time to provide services at a proper time and by an appropriate mode so as not to impede operations of other service providers;

2. To carry out any necessary cooperation with other service providers.

TIME LIMIT FOR COMPLETION OF SERVICES

1. Service providers must complete their services within the time limits already agreed upon in contracts.

2. Where there is no agreement on the time limits for completing services, service providers shall have to complete their services within a reasonable time limit on the basis of taking into account all conditions and circumstances which service providers knew at the time the contracts were entered into, including any specific needs of customers regarding such time limit for service completion.

3. Where a service can be completed only when the customer or another service provider satisfies certain conditions, the provider of such service is not obliged to complete his/her service until those conditions are satisfied.

CUSTOMERS' REQUESTS FOR CHANGES DURING THE PROVISION OF SERVICES

1. During the provision of services, service providers must satisfy all reasonable requests of their customers for changes during the provision of services.

2. Unless otherwise agreed, customers must bear reasonable expenses for the satisfaction of their requests for changes.

CONTINUED PROVISION OF SERVICES AFTER THE EXPIRATION OF THE TIME LIMIT FOR COMPLETING THE PROVISION OF SERVICES

If services, after the expiration of the time limit for completing the provision thereof, are not yet completed, and if customers have no objection, service providers shall have to continue providing the agreed services and compensate for damage, if any.

OBLIGATIONS OF CUSTOMERS

Unless otherwise agreed, customers shall have the following obligations:

1. To pay charges for provision of services as agreed upon in contracts;

2. To provide in a timely manner plans, instructions and other details so that the provision of services can be made without any delay or interruption;

3. To cooperate with service providers in all other matters necessary for the proper provision of services;

4. Where a service is performed jointly by many service providers or by a provider in coordination with other service providers, customers shall be obliged to coordinate operations of these service providers so as not to impede the work of any service provider.

SERVICE CHARGE RATE

Where there is no agreement on service charge rate, no agreement on methods of determining service charge rate, and also there is not any indication to service charge rate, the service charge rate shall be determined according to the charge rate of the same type of service under similar conditions on mode of provision, time of provision, geographical market, mode of payment and other conditions which can affect the service charge rate.

TIME LIMIT FOR PAYMENT

Where there is no agreement and there exist no customs pre-established between the parties concerning payment for services, the time limit for payment shall be the time when the provision of services is completed.

SALE PROMOTION

1. Sale promotion means activities of commercial promotion conducted by traders to promote the purchase and sale of goods or the provision of services by offering certain benefits to customers.

2. Traders conducting sale promotion are those falling into one of the following cases:

a/ Traders directly conduct sale promotion for goods and/or services that they trade in;

b/ Traders engaged in providing sale promotion services conduct sale promotion for goods and/or services of other traders under an agreement with the latter.

PROVISION OF SALE PROMOTION SERVICE

Provision of sale promotion services means commercial activities whereby a trader conducts sale promotion for goods and/or services of other traders on a contractual basis.

SALE PROMOTION SERVICE CONTRACTS

Sale promotion service contracts must be made in writing or in other forms of equal legal validity.

FORMS OF SALE PROMOTION

1. Giving samples of goods or providing samples of services to customers for trial use free of charge.

2. Presenting goods as gifts or providing free-of-charge services to customers.

3. Selling goods or providing services at prices lower than goods sale prices or service provision charge rates previously applied during the period of sale promotion already registered or announced. In case of goods or services subject to the State management over their prices, the sale promotion in this form shall comply with regulations of the Government.

4. Selling goods or providing services together with coupons that allow customers to enjoy one or several benefits.

5. Selling goods or providing services together with prize-contest entrance tickets to customers, for purpose of selecting prize winners according to the rules and prizes already announced.

6. Selling goods or providing services together with opportunities for customers to participate in games of chance, the participation in which comes after the purchase of goods or services and the winning of prizes depends on the luck of participants according to the rules and prizes already announced.

7. Organizing programs for frequent customers whereby gifts are presented to customers on the basis of the quantities or values of goods purchased or services used by such customers and expressed in forms of customers' cards, coupons acknowledging the purchase of goods or services, or other forms.

8. Organizing cultural, artistic or entertainment programs or other events for customers for the purpose of sale promotion.

9. Other forms of sale promotion if approved by the State management agency in charge of commerce.

SALE PROMOTION GOODS AND SERVICES

1. Sale promotion goods and services mean goods and services use by traders to promote their sale and provision in various forms of sale promotion.

2. Sale promotion goods and services must be those traded lawfully.

GOODS AND SERVICES USED FOR SALE PROMOTION, SALE PROMOTION DISCOUNT RATES

1. Goods and services used for sale promotion mean those given as gifts or prizes or provided free of charge by traders to customers.

2. Goods and services used by traders for sale promotion may be goods and services they are trading in or other goods and services.

3. Goods and services used for sale promotion must be those traded lawfully.

4. The Government shall specify the maximum value of goods and services used for sale promotion, and the maximum discount rate for sale promotion goods and services, which traders can apply in their sale promotion activities.

RIGHTS OF TRADERS CONDUCTING SALE PROMOTION

1. To choose the form, time and venue for sale promotion, goods and services to be used for sale promotion.

2. To hire traders engaged in the business of providing sale promotion services to conduct sale promotion for them.

3. To organize the application of the sale promotion forms specified in commercial law.

KEEPING SECRET INFORMATION ON SALE PROMOTION PROGRAMS AND DETAILS

Where sale promotion programs must be approved by competent state agencies, such agencies must keep secret the sale promotion programs and details provided by traders until such programs are approved by competent state agencies.

PROHIBITED ACTS IN SALE PROMOTION ACTIVITIES

1. Conducting sale promotion for goods and services banned from business; goods and services subject to business restrictions; goods not yet permitted for circulation; and services not yet permitted for provision;

2. Using, for sale promotion purpose, goods and services which are banned from business; goods and services subject to business restrictions; goods not yet permitted for circulation; and services not yet permitted for provision;

3. Conducting sale promotion for alcohol and beer, or using alcohol and beer for sale promotion targeted at under-18 people;

4. Conducting sale promotion for, or using cigarette or alcohol of an alcoholic volume of 30o or higher for sale promotion in any form;

5. Conducting untruthful or misleading sale promotion for goods and services so as to deceive customers;

6. Conducting sale promotion for selling inferior-quality goods, causing harms to the environment, human health and other public interests;

7. Conducting sale promotion at schools, hospitals or offices of state agencies, political organizations, socio-political organizations and people's armed forces units;

8. Promising to present gifts or prizes but failing to do so or doing it improperly;

9. Conducting sale promotion for purpose of unfair competition;

REGISTRATION FOR SALE PROMOTION ACTIVITIES WITH, AND NOTIFICATION OF SALE PROMOTION RESULTS TO, THE STATE MANAGEMENT AGENCY IN CHARGE OF COMMERCE

1. Before conducting sale promotion activities, traders must register them with the state management agency in charge of commerce, and after such sale promotion activities are completed, report sale promotion results to such agency.

2. The Government shall provide for in detail the registration of sale promotion activities with, and the notification of results of such activities to, the state management agency in charge of commerce.

COMMERCIAL ADVERTISING

Commercial advertising means commercial promotion activities of traders aimed at introducing to customers their goods and service business activities.

PROVISION OF COMMERCIAL ADVERTISING SERVICES

Provision of commercial advertising services means commercial activities of traders aimed at conducting commercial advertisement for other traders.

COMMERCIAL ADVERTISING PRODUCTS

Commercial advertising products consist of information in images, actions, sounds, voices, scripts, symbols, colors and lights containing commercial advertising details.

MEANS OF COMMERCIAL ADVERTISING

1. Means of commercial advertising are instruments used for introducing commercial advertising products.

2. Means of commercial advertising include:

a/ The mass media;

b/ Means of communications;

c/ Publications of all kinds;

d/ All kinds of boards, signs, banners, panels, posters, fixed objects or means of transportation and other movable objects;

e/ Other means of commercial advertising.

USE OF MEANS OF COMMERCIAL ADVERTISING

1. The use of means of commercial advertising must comply with the regulations of the competent state management body.

2. The use of means of commercial advertising must satisfy the following requirements:

a/ Being in compliance with the provisions of law on press, publishing, information, programs on cultural or sport activities, trade fairs and exhibitions;

b/ Being in compliance with the regulations on locations of advertisement, causing no adverse impact on the landscape, environment, traffic order and safety, and social safety;

c/ Being in accordance with the intensity, time volume and timing prescribed for each type of mass media.

PROTECTION OF INTELLECTUAL PROPERTY RIGHTS OVER COMMERCIAL ADVERTISING PRODUCTS

Traders shall have the right to register for protection of their intellectual property rights over commercial advertising products according to the provisions of law.

PROHIBITED COMMERCIAL ADVERTISEMENTS

1. Advertisements which reveal state secrets, are detrimental to the national independence, sovereignty and security, and social order and safety.

2. Advertisements that use advertising products or means of advertisement which are contrary to the historic, cultural and ethical traditions.

3. Advertisements for goods and services which are banned or restricted from business or banned from advertisement by the State.

4. Commercial advertisements which can be taken advantage of to cause harms to interests of the State, organizations and/or individuals.

5. Advertisements using the method of comparing a trader's goods and service production and business activities with goods and service production and business activities of the same kind of other traders.

6. Advertisements containing untruthful information on any of the following contents: quantity, quality, price, utility, design, origin, category, packing, service mode and warranty duration of goods or services.

7. Advertisements for a trader's business activities by using advertising products which infringe upon intellectual property rights; using images of other organizations or individuals for advertising purpose without the consent of such organizations or individuals.

8. Advertisements for the purpose of unfair competition according to the provisions of law.

COMMERCIAL ADVERTISING SERVICE CONTRACTS

Commercial advertising service contracts must be made in writing or in other forms of equivalent legal validity.

RIGHTS OF COMMERCIAL ADVERTISING HIRERS

Unless otherwise agreed, commercial advertising hirers shall have the following rights:

1. To select commercial advertising distributors, forms, contents, means, scope and duration;

2. To inspect and supervise the performance of commercial advertising service contracts.

OBLIGATIONS OF COMMERCIAL ADVERTISING HIRERS

Unless otherwise agreed, commercial advertising hirers shall have the following obligations:

1. To supply commercial advertising service providers with truthful and accurate information on goods and commercial service business activities, and to be responsible for such information;

2. To pay commercial advertising service charges and other reasonable costs.

RIGHTS OF COMMERCIAL ADVERTISING SERVICE PROVIDERS

Unless otherwise agreed, commercial advertising service providers shall have the following rights:

1. To request commercial advertising hirers to supply truthful and accurate information according to agreements in contracts;

2. To receive commercial advertising service charges and other reasonable costs.

OBLIGATIONS OF COMMERCIAL ADVERTISING SERVICE PROVIDERS

Unless otherwise agreed, commercial advertising service providers shall have the following obligations:

1. To comply with service hirers' choice of commercial advertising distributors, forms, contents, means, scope and duration;

2. To organize truthful and accurate advertisement for goods or commercial service business activities according to information supplied by advertising hirers;

3. To perform other obligations agreed upon in commercial advertising service contracts.

COMMERCIAL ADVERTISING DISTRIBUTORS

Commercial advertising distributors are persons who directly distribute commercial advertising products.

OBLIGATIONS OF COMMERCIAL ADVERTISING DISTRIBUTORS

Commercial advertising distributors shall have the following obligations:

1. To comply with the provisions of commercial law on the use of means of commercial advertising;

2. To perform advertising distribution contracts already entered into with advertising distribution hirers;

3. To perform other obligations provided for by law.

DISPLAY AND INTRODUCTION OF GOODS AND SERVICES

Display and introduction of goods and services mean commercial promotion activities of traders that use goods and/or services and documents thereon to introduce such goods and/or services to customers.

PROVISION OF GOODS/SERVICE DISPLAY AND INTRODUCTION SERVICES

Provision of goods/service display and introduction services means commercial activities whereby a trader provides goods/service display and introduction services to other traders.

FORMS OF DISPLAY AND INTRODUCTION OF GOODS AND SERVICES

1. Opening showrooms for displaying and introducing goods and/or services.

2. Displaying and introducing goods and/or services at trade centers or in entertainment, sport, cultural or artistic activities.

3. Organizing conferences and seminars involving the display and introduction of goods and/or services.

4. Displaying and introducing goods and/or services online and in other forms specified by law.

CONDITIONS FOR DISPLAYED AND INTRODUCED GOODS AND/OR SERVICES

1. Displayed and introduced goods and/or services must be those which are legally traded in the market.

2. Displayed and introduced goods and/or services must comply with the provisions of law on goods quality and goods labeling.

CASES WHERE DISPLAY AND INTRODUCTION OF GOODS AND/OR SERVICES ARE PROHIBITED

1. The organization of display and introduction of goods and/or services, or the use of forms and means of goods and/or service display and introduction, which are detrimental to national security, social order and safety, landscape, environment and human health;

2. Display and introduction of goods and/or services or use of forms and means of display and introduction, which are contrary to the historic, cultural and ethical traditions and fine customs;

3. Display and introduction of goods and/or services, which reveal state secrets;

4. Display and introduction of goods of other traders for comparison with one's own goods, except where the goods for comparison are counterfeit goods or goods infringing upon intellectual property rights according to the provisions of law;

5. Display and introduction of goods samples which are inconsistent with goods being traded in terms of quality, price, utility, design, category, packing, warranty duration and other quality standards in order to deceive customers.

CONTRACTS FOR PROVISION OF GOODS AND/OR SERVICE DISPLAY AND INTRODUCTION SERVICES

Contracts for provision of goods and/or service display and introduction services must be made in writing or in other forms of equivalent legal validity.

RIGHTS OF GOODS AND/OR SERVICE DISPLAY AND INTRODUCTION SERVICE HIRERS

Unless otherwise agreed, goods and/or service display and introduction service hirers shall have the following rights:

1. To request goods and/or service display and introduction service providers to fulfill agreements in contracts;

2. To inspect and supervise the performance of goods and/or service display and introduction service contracts.

OBLIGATIONS OF GOODS AND/OR SERVICE DISPLAY AND INTRODUCTION SERVICE HIRERS

Unless otherwise agreed, goods and/or service display and introduction service hirers shall have the following obligations:

1. To supply all goods and/or services to be displayed and introduced, or means to service providers as agreed upon in contracts;

2. To supply information on goods and/or services to be displayed and introduced and take responsibility for such information;

3. To pay service charges and other reasonable expenses.

RIGHTS OF GOODS AND/OR SERVICE DISPLAY AND INTRODUCTION SERVICE PROVIDERS

Unless otherwise agreed, goods and/or service display and introduction service providers shall have the following rights:

1. To request service hirers to supply goods and/or services to be displayed and introduced within time limits agreed upon in contracts;

2. To request service hirers to supply information on goods and/or services to be displayed and introduced and other necessary means as agreed upon in contracts;

3. To receive service charges and other reasonable expenses.

OBLIGATIONS OF GOODS AND/OR SERVICE DISPLAY AND INTRODUCTION SERVICE PROVIDERS

Unless otherwise agreed, goods and/or service display and introduction service providers shall have the following obligations:

1. To display and introduce goods and/or services as agreed upon in contracts;

2. To preserve displayed and introduced goods, documents and means supplied to them during the performance of contracts; and upon the completion of the goods and/or service display and introduction, to return all displayed and introduced goods, documents and means to service hirers;

3. To conduct the goods and/or service display and introduction according to contents agreed with service hirers.

TRADE FAIRS AND EXHIBITIONS

Trade fairs and exhibitions mean commercial promotion activities conducted in a concentrated manner at particular locations and for given periods of time for traders to display and introduce their goods and/or services for the purpose of promoting them and seeking opportunities for entering into contracts for sale and purchase of goods or service contracts.

PROVISION OF TRADE FAIR AND EXHIBITION SERVICES

1. Provision of trade fair and exhibition services means commercial activities whereby traders dealing in these services provide services of organizing or participating in trade fairs and exhibitions to other traders for receiving trade fair and exhibition organization service charges.

2. Trade fair and exhibition organization service contracts must be made in writing or in other forms of equivalent legal validity.

ORGANIZATION OF AND PARTICIPATION IN OVERSEAS TRADE FAIRS AND EXHIBITIONS

1. Traders not providing trade fair and exhibition services, when directly organizing or participating in overseas trade fairs and exhibitions for goods and/or services they trade in, must comply with the regulations on export of goods.

2. Traders providing trade fair and exhibition services, when arranging for other traders to participate in overseas trade fairs and exhibitions, must register such with the Ministry of Trade.

3. Traders that have not yet registered their business of providing trade fair and exhibition services shall not be allowed to arrange for other traders to participate in overseas trade fairs and exhibitions.

GOODS AND/OR SERVICES PARTICIPATING IN OVERSEAS TRADE FAIRS AND EXHIBITIONS

1. All types of goods and services shall be permitted to participate in overseas trade fairs and exhibitions, except for those banned from export according to the provisions of law.

2. Goods and/or services banned from export shall only be permitted for participation in overseas trade fairs and exhibitions when so approved by the Prime Minister.

3. The time limit for temporary export of goods for participation in overseas trade fairs and exhibitions shall be one year from the date such goods are temporarily exported.

4. The temporary export for re-import of goods for participation in overseas trade fairs and exhibitions must comply with the provisions of customs law and other relevant provisions of law.

RIGHTS AND OBLIGATIONS OF ORGANIZATIONS AND INDIVIDUALS PARTICIPATING IN TRADE FAIRS AND EXHIBITIONS.

1. To exercise rights and perform obligations as agreed upon with traders organizing trade fairs and exhibitions.

2. To sell, present goods as gifts and provide services displayed and introduced at trade fairs and exhibitions according to the provisions of law.

3. To temporarily import and re-export goods and documents on goods and/or services for display at trade fairs and exhibitions.

4. To comply with regulations on organization of trade fairs and exhibitions.

RIGHTS AND OBLIGATIONS OF TRADERS ORGANIZING OR PARTICIPATING IN OVERSEAS TRADE FAIRS AND EXHIBITIONS

1. To temporarily export and re-import goods and documents on goods and/or services for display and introduction at trade fairs or exhibitions.

2. To comply with regulations on organization of, and participation in, overseas trade fairs and exhibitions.

3. To sell and present as gifts goods displayed and introduced at overseas trade fairs and exhibitions; and to pay taxes and fulfill other financial obligations as provided for by law.

RIGHTS AND OBLIGATIONS OF TRADERS PROVIDING TRADE FAIR AND EXHIBITION SERVICES

1. To post up topics and durations of trade fairs and exhibitions at places where such trade fairs and exhibitions are to be organized before their opening dates.

2. To request service hirers to supply goods for participation in trade fairs and exhibitions within time limits agreed upon in contracts.

3. To request service hirers to supply information on goods and/or services for participation in trade fairs and exhibitions and other necessary means as agreed upon in contracts;

4. To receive service charges and other reasonable expenses;

5. To organize trade fairs and exhibitions as agreed upon in contracts.

AGREEMENT ON REPRESENTATION FOR TRADERS

An agreement on representation for traders must be in writing or take other forms which have the same legal value.

SCOPE OF REPRESENTATION

Contracting parties may reach an agreement where the representative is authorized to represent, whether in part or in whole, trading activities that fall within the remit of the principal.

DURATION OF REPRESENTATION FOR TRADERS

1. Duration of representation shall be agreed upon by contracting parties.

2. In the absence of any agreement, the validity duration of representation ends in either case where the principal or the representative notifies the other of termination of the representation agreement.

OBLIGATIONS OF THE REPRESENTATIVE

Unless otherwise agreed, the representative shall take on the following obligations:

1. Perform trades under the name, and for the interests of, the principal;

2. Inform the principal of opportunities for, and outcomes of, performance of trades which have been authorized;

3. Observe the principal's instructions which are not in violation of laws and regulations.

4. Avoid performing trades under the name of his/her own or of any third party within the scope of representation;

5. Avoid disclosing or providing any non-party confidential information about his/her trades during the validity duration when his/her representation is rendered and within two years after that representation agreement is terminated;

6. Provide safe custody of assets or documents which have been entrusted to perform representation activities.

OBLIGATIONS OF THE PRINCIPAL

Unless otherwise agreed, the principal shall assume the following obligations:

1. Promptly inform the representative of conclusion of contracts that the representative has negotiated, execution of contracts that the representative has negotiated, approval or rejection of activities which do not fall within the agreed remit of the representative;

2. Provide assets, documents and any information necessary for the representative's contractual representation activities;

3. Pay remunerations and other reasonable expenses to the representative;

4. Duly inform the representative of possibility that a contract may not be concluded or executed within the stated scope of representation.

PAYMENT FOR ANY EXPENSE INCURRED

Unless otherwise agreed, the representative shall be accorded the right to claim payments for any expense incurred on a reasonable basis for the purpose of performing contractual representation activities.

LIEN

Unless otherwise agreed, the representative shall be entitled to exercise lien over entrusted assets and documents to secure the payment of remunerations and expenses due.

COMMERCIAL BROKERAGE

Commercial brokerage means a commercial activity whereby a trader acts as an intermediary (referred to as broker) between parties selling and purchasing goods or providing commercial services (referred to as principals) in the course of negotiations and entering into contracts for sale and purchase of goods or provision of services and shall be entitled to a remuneration under a brokerage contract.

OBLIGATIONS OF COMMERCIAL BROKERS

Unless otherwise agreed, a commercial broker shall have the following obligations:

1. To preserve samples of goods and documents assigned for the performance of brokerage activities, and to return them to the principals after the completion of brokerage;

2. Not to disclose or supply information to the detriment of the interests of the principals;

3. To be responsible for the legal status, but not for the solvency, of the principals;

4. Not to take part in the performance of contracts between the principals, except where so authorized by the principals.

OBLIGATIONS OF PRINCIPALS

Unless otherwise agreed, a principal shall have the following obligations:

1. To supply information, documents, necessary means related to goods and services;

2. To pay brokerage remuneration and other reasonable expenses to the broker.

THE RIGHT TO ENJOY BROKERAGE REMUNERATION

Unless otherwise agreed, the right to enjoy brokerage remuneration arises from the time the principals enter into contracts.

PAYMENT OF EXPENSES INCURRED IN RELATION TO BROKERAGE

Unless otherwise agreed, principals must pay all reasonable expenses incurred in relation to brokerage to brokers, even where the brokerage does not bring about any results for principals.

PURCHASE AND SALE OF GOODS BY MANDATED DEALERS

Purchase and sale of goods by mandated dealers mean commercial activities whereby the mandatory conducts the purchase and sale of goods in his/her/its own name under terms agreed upon with the mandator and is entitled to receive mandate commission.

MANDATORIES

A mandatory for purchase and sale of goods is a trader dealing in goods which are consistent with the mandated goods and conducting the purchase and sale of goods under terms agreed upon with the mandator.

MANDATORS

A mandator of purchase and sale of goods may, or may not, be a trader that authorizes a mandatory to conduct the purchase and sale of goods at his/her/its request and pays a commission.

MANDATED GOODS

All goods which are lawfully circulated may become the subject matter of a mandated sale and purchase.

MANDATE CONTRACTS

Mandate contracts for purchase and sale of goods must be made in writing or in other forms of equivalent legal validity.

SUB-MANDATE TO A THIRD PARTY

A mandatory shall not be allowed to sub-mandate a third party to perform the signed mandate contract for purchase and sale of goods, except where it is so approved in writing by the mandator.

MULTILATERAL MANDATE

A mandatory may accept the mandate for purchase and sale of goods from different mandators.

RIGHTS OF MANDATORS

Unless otherwise agreed, mandators shall have the following rights:

1. To request mandatories to supply adequate information on the performance of mandate contracts;

2. Not to bear responsibility in cases where mandatories commit law violations.

OBLIGATIONS OF MANDATORS

Unless otherwise agreed, mandators shall have the following obligations:

1. To provide information, documents and means necessary for the performance of mandate contracts;

2. To pay mandate commissions and other reasonable expenses to mandatories;

3. To hand over money and goods as agreed upon;

4. To bear joint responsibility in cases where mandatories commit law violations which are attributable to acts of mandators or intentional law-breaking acts of the parties.

RIGHTS OF MANDATORIES

Unless otherwise agreed, mandatories shall have the following rights:

1. To request mandators to provide information and documents necessary for the performance of mandate contracts;

2. To receive mandate commissions;

3. Not to bear responsibility for goods handed over to mandators strictly under agreement.

OBLIGATIONS OF MANDATORIES

Unless otherwise agreed, mandatories shall have the following obligations:

1. To conduct the purchase and sale of goods as agreed upon;

2. To notify mandators of matters related to the performance of mandate contracts;

3. To follow instructions of mandators as agreed upon;

4. To preserve assets and documents assigned to them for the performance of mandate contracts;

5. To keep secret information related to the performance of mandate contracts;

6. To hand over money and goods as agreed upon;

7. To bear joint responsibility for law violation acts of mandators, in cases where such law violation acts are partially attributable to their own faults.

COMMERCIAL AGENCY

Commercial agency means a commercial activity whereby the principal and the agent agree that the agent, in its own name, sells or purchases goods for the principal or provides services of the principal to customers for remuneration.

PRINCIPALS AND AGENTS

1. Principals are traders that deliver goods to agents for sale or provide money to agents for purchase of goods, or traders that authorize the provision of services to service-providing agents.

2. Agents are traders that receive goods to act as sale agents or receive money to act as purchase agents or accepts the authorization to provide services.

AGENCY CONTRACTS

Agency contracts must be made in writing or in other forms of equivalent legal validity.

FORMS OF AGENCY

1. Off-take agency is a form of agency whereby the agent definitely sells or purchases a specific quantity of goods or provides a full service for the principal.

2. Exclusive agency is a form of agency whereby a sole agent is authorized by the principal to sell or purchase one or more goods items or to provide one or more types of services within a given geographical area.

3. General goods sale or purchase or service provision agency is a form of agency whereby an agent organizes a network of sub-agents to sell or purchase goods, or provide services for the principal.

The general agent represents the network of sub-agents. Sub-agents operate under the management and in the name of the general agent.

4. Other forms of agency agreed upon by the parties.

OWNERSHIP RIGHT IN COMMERCIAL AGENCY

The principal is the owner of goods or money delivered to the agent(s).

AGENCY REMUNERATION

1. Unless otherwise agreed, agency remuneration shall be paid to agents in the form of commission or price margin.

2. Where principals fix goods purchase or sale prices or service charge rates, agents shall enjoy commissions calculated in percentage of such goods purchase or sale prices or service charge rates.

3. Where principals do not fix goods purchase or sale prices or service charge rates but fix only agency prices, agents shall enjoy price margins. Price margin is determined to be the difference between goods purchase or sale price or service charge rate and the price fixed by the principals for the agent.

4. Where the parties do not agree upon the agency remuneration level, the remuneration level shall be calculated as follows:

a/ The actual remuneration level which has been previously paid by/to parties;

b/ Where Point a of this Clause cannot apply, the agency remuneration level shall be the average remuneration level applicable to the same type of goods or service paid by the principal to other agents;

c/ Where Points a and b of this Clause cannot apply, the agency remuneration level shall be the ordinary remuneration level applicable to the same type of goods or service in the market.

RIGHTS OF PRINCIPALS

Unless otherwise agreed, principals shall have the following rights:

1. To fix prices of goods purchased or sold or charge rates of services provided to customers under agency;

2. To fix agency prices;

3. To request agents to take security measures as provided for by law;

4. To request agents to make payments or deliver goods under agency contracts;

5. To inspect and supervise the performance of contracts by agents;

OBLIGATIONS OF PRINCIPALS

Unless otherwise agreed, principals shall have the following obligations:

1. To guide, supply information to, and facilitate, agents to perform agency contracts;

2. To bear responsibility for quality of goods of goods sale or purchase agents, and quality of services of service-providing agents;

3. To pay remuneration and other reasonable expenses to agents;

4. To return to agents their assets used as security (if any) upon the termination of agency contracts;

5. To bear joint responsibility for law violation acts of agents if such law violation acts are partly attributable to their faults.

RIGHTS OF AGENTS

Unless otherwise agreed by the parties, agents shall have the following rights:

1. To enter into agency contracts with one or more principals;

2. To request principals to deliver goods or money under agency contracts; to take back assets used as security (if any) upon the termination of agency contracts;

3. To request principals to guide, supply information and create other related conditions for the performance of agency contracts;

4. To decide on goods sale prices or service charge rates for customers, for off-take agents;

5. To enjoy remunerations and other lawful rights and interests brought about by agency activities.

OBLIGATIONS OF AGENTS

Unless otherwise agreed, agents shall have the following obligations:

1. To purchase or sell goods or provide services to customers at prices or charge rates fixed by principals;

2. To comply strictly with agreements on handover and receipt of money and goods with principals;

3. To take security measures for performance of civil obligations as provided for by law;

4. To pay to principals any proceeds of the sale of goods, for sale agents; to deliver purchased goods to principals, for purchase agents; or to pay service charges to principals, for service-providing agents;

5. To preserve goods after the receipt thereof, for sale agents, or prior to the delivery thereof, for purchase agents; to bear joint responsibility for quality of goods of purchase or sale agents or quality of services of service-providing agents in cases where they are at fault;

6. To submit to inspection and supervision by principals, and to report to principals on their agency activities;

7. Where it is specified by law that an agent shall be allowed to enter into an agency contract with a principal for a certain type of goods or service, such provision of law must be complied with.

PAYMENT IN AGENCY ACTIVITIES

Unless otherwise agreed, payments for goods, payment of service charges and payment of agency remunerations shall be made in installments after agents complete the purchase or sale of a specific quantity of goods or the provision of a specific volume of services.

LOGISTIC SERVICES

Logistic services are commercial activities whereby traders organize the performance of one or many jobs including reception, transportation, warehousing, yard storage of cargoes, completion of customs procedures and other formalities and paperwork, provision of consultancy to customers, services of packaging, marking, delivery of goods, or other services related to goods according to agreements with customers in order to enjoy service charges.

CONDITIONS FOR LOGISTIC SERVICE PROVISION

1. Traders providing logistic services are enterprises fully satisfying the conditions for logistic service business provided for by law.

2. The Government shall specify logistic service business conditions.

RIGHTS AND OBLIGATIONS OF TRADERS PROVIDING LOGISTIC SERVICES

1. Unless otherwise agreed, traders providing logistic services shall have the following rights and obligations:

a/ To enjoy service charges and other reasonable expenses;

b/ To depart from instructions of customers during the performance of contracts for plausible reasons and in the interests of customers, provided that customers must be notified thereof immediately;

c/ To notify such customers immediately for further instructions in cases where instructions of customers cannot be followed in part or in whole;

d/ To perform their obligations within a reasonable period of time if there is no agreement on specific time limit for performance of their obligations to customers.

2. In the course of transportations of goods, traders providing logistic services must comply with the provisions of law and transportation practices.

RIGHTS AND OBLIGATIONS OF CUSTOMERS

Unless otherwise agreed, customers shall have the following rights and obligations:

1. To guide, inspect and supervise the performance of contracts;

2. To provide sufficient instructions to traders providing logistic services;

3. To provide sufficient, detailed and accurate information on the goods to traders providing logistic services;

4. To pack and mark the goods according to contracts for purchase and sale of goods, except where there is an agreement that traders providing logistic services shall undertake to do such job;

5. To compensate for damage caused to, and pay reasonable costs incurred by, traders providing logistic services if such traders have strictly complied with customers' instructions or if the customers are at fault;

6. To pay traders providing logistic services all amounts due.

LIABILITY EXEMPTION FOR TRADERS PROVIDING LOGISTIC SERVICES

1. Apart from the cases of liability exemption specified in commercial law, traders providing logistic services shall not be liable for the goods loss caused in the following cases:

a/ The loss is caused by faults of customers or their authorized persons;

b/ The loss is caused by traders that have strictly followed the instructions of their customers or persons authorized by customers;

c/ The loss is attributed to defects of the goods;

d/ The loss occurs in cases of liability exemption according to law and transportation practices, if traders providing logistic services organize transportation;

e/ Trader providing logistic services are not notified of complaints within fourteen days from the date they deliver goods to recipients;

f/ After being complained against, traders providing logistic services are not notified of lawsuits against them being instituted at arbitrations or courts within nine months from the date of delivery of goods.

2. Traders providing logistic services shall not be liable for the loss of profits which their customers would have earned, for any services delayed or provided at wrong addresses, for which they are not at fault.

LIMITATION TO LIABILITY

1. Unless otherwise agreed, the full liability of traders providing logistic services shall not exceed the limitation of liability for the full loss of the goods.

2. The Government shall provide in detail for the limitation of liability of traders providing logistic services in compliance with provisions of law and international practices.

3. Traders providing logistic services shall not enjoy the limitation of liability for damage compensation if persons with related rights and benefits prove that the loss, damage or delayed delivery of goods is caused by deliberate actions or inactions of traders providing logistic services with the intention to cause such loss, damage or delayed delivery or their actions or inactions are known to be risky who were also aware of such loss, damage, or delay would certainly occur.

THE RIGHT TO WITHHOLD AND DISPOSE OF GOODS

1. Traders providing logistic services shall be entitled to withhold a certain quantity of goods and related documents in order to claim payment of due debts by customers but shall have to notify promptly customers thereof in writing.

2. After forty-five days from the date of notification of the withholding of goods or their related documents, if customers fail to pay debts, traders providing logistic services shall be entitled to dispose of such goods or documents according to provisions of law. Where there are indications of deterioration of goods, traders providing logistic services shall have the right to dispose of the goods immediately after any debt of customers becomes due.

3. Before disposing of goods, traders providing logistic services must immediately notify their customers of such disposal.

4. All expenses for the withholding and disposal of goods shall be borne by customers.

5. Traders providing logistic services shall be entitled to use proceeds from the disposal of goods to pay for debts owed to them by their customers and related expenses. If the proceeds from the disposal of goods exceed the value of debts, the difference must be returned to customers. From that point of time, traders providing logistic services shall no longer be responsible for the goods or documents already disposed of.

OBLIGATIONS OF TRADERS PROVIDING LOGISTIC SERVICES WHEN WITHHOLDING GOODS

When the right to dispose of goods is not yet exercised, traders providing logistic services and withholding goods shall have the following obligations:

1. To preserve and keep the goods;

2. Not to use goods without consent of the parties whose goods are withheld;

3. To return goods where the conditions for withholding and disposal of goods no longer exist;

4. To pay damages to the parties whose goods are withheld if they cause loss or damage to withheld goods.

TRANSIT OF GOODS

Transit of goods means the transportation of goods owned by foreign organizations or individuals through the territory, including transshipment, portage, warehousing, shipment separation or alteration of modes of transportation or other jobs performed in the course of transit.

RIGHT TO TRANSIT GOODS

All goods owned by foreign organizations and individuals are allowed to be transited through the territory and subject only to customs clearance at import border-gates and export border-gates according to the provisions of law, except for the following cases:

a/ Goods are weapons, ammunitions, explosive materials and other type of highly dangerous goods;

b/ Goods are banned from business, export or import, which shall be allowed to be transited through the territory only.

PROHIBITED ACTS DURING TRANSIT

1. To pay transit remunerations in transit goods.

2. To illegally consume goods in transit or means of transport carrying goods in transit.

GOODS TRANSIT SERVICES

Goods transit services mean commercial activities whereby traders carry out the transit of goods under the ownership of foreign organizations or individuals through the territory for remunerations.

TRANSIT SERVICE CONTRACTS

Transit service contracts must be made in writing or in other forms of equivalent legal validity.

RIGHTS AND OBLIGATIONS OF TRANSIT SERVICE HIRERS

1. Unless otherwise agreed, transit service hirers shall have the following rights:

a/ To request transit service providers to receive goods at import border-gates at the agreed time;

b/ To request transit service providers to promptly notify the conditions of goods in the course of transit through the territory;

c/ To request transit service providers to carry out all necessary procedures to limit damage or loss of goods in transit in the course of transit through the territory.

2. Unless otherwise agreed, transit service hirers shall have the following obligations:

a/ To supply transit service providers with sufficient information on the goods;

b/ To supply sufficient documents necessary for transit service providers to carry out procedures for import or transportation in the territory and the export procedures;

c/ To pay transit remunerations and other reasonable expenses to transit service providers.

ASSESSMENT SERVICES

Assessment services are commercial activities whereby traders perform necessary jobs to determine actual conditions of goods, results of the provision of services and other contents at the request of customers.

CONTENTS OF ASSESSMENT

Assessment comprises one or a number of contents regarding the quantity, quality, packing, value of goods, origin of goods, losses, safety, hygienic and quarantine standards, results of the provision of services, method of providing services and other contents at the request of customers.

TRADERS PROVIDING COMMERCIAL ASSESSMENT SERVICES

Only traders that satisfy all the conditions provided for by law and are granted business registration certificates for provision of commercial assessment services shall be allowed to provide assessment services and issue assessment certificates.

CRITERIA OF ASSESSORS

An assessor must fully satisfy the following criteria:

a/ Possessing a university or college degree suitable to the requirements of the domain of assessment;

b/ Having a professional certificate for the assessment domain in cases where such professional certificate is required by law;

c/ Having worked for at least three years in the domain of assessment of goods or services.

ASSESSMENT CERTIFICATES

1. Assessment certificates are documents determining the actual conditions of goods and services according to the assessment contents required by customers.

2. Assessment certificates must be signed by competent representatives of enterprises providing commercial assessment services, have signatures and full names of assessors, and be affixed with professional seals already registered with competent agencies.

3. Assessment certificates shall only be valid for those contents already assessed.

4. Traders providing assessment services shall be responsible for accuracy of results and conclusions in assessment certificates.

LEGAL VALIDITY OF ASSESSMENT CERTIFICATES WITH RESPECT TO ASSESSMENT REQUESTERS

Assessment certificates shall be legally binding on assessment requesters in cases where they cannot prove that assessment results are non-objective, untruthful or obtained with technical or professional errors.

RIGHTS AND OBLIGATIONS OF TRADERS PROVIDING ASSESSMENT SERVICES

1. Traders providing assessment services shall have the following rights:

a/ To request customers to supply in a sufficient, accurate and timely manner necessary documents for performance of assessment services;

b/ To receive assessment service charges and other reasonable expenses.

2. Traders providing assessment services shall have the following obligations:

a/ To observe the standards and other relevant provisions of law on assessment services;

b/ To perform the assessment in an honest, objective, independent, timely manner and according to the assessment procedures and methods;

c/ To issue assessment certificates;

d/ To pay violation fines and/or damages.

RIGHTS OF CUSTOMERS

Unless otherwise agreed, customers shall have the following rights:

1. To request traders providing assessment services to perform the assessment according to the agreed contents;

2. To request re-assessment if they have sound reasons to believe that traders providing assessment services fail to properly satisfy their requirements or perform the assessment in an untruthful and non-objective manner or with technical and professional errors;

3. To request payment of fines or damages.

OBLIGATIONS OF CUSTOMERS

Unless otherwise agreed, customers shall have the following obligations:

1. To supply in a sufficient, accurate and timely manner necessary documents to traders providing assessment services when so requested;

2. To pay assessment service charges and other reasonable expenses.

FINES AND DAMAGES IN CASE OF INCORRECT ASSESSMENT RESULTS

1. Where traders providing assessment services issue assessment certificates showing incorrect results caused by their unintentional faults, they must pay fines therefor to customers. The fine level shall be agreed upon by the parties but must not exceed ten times the assessment service charge.

2. Where traders providing assessment services issue assessment certificates showing incorrect results caused by their intentional faults, they must pay compensations for damage caused to customers that directly request the assessment.

3. Customers are obliged to prove that assessment results are incorrect and traders providing assessment services are at fault.

ASSESSMENT AT THE REQUEST OF STATE AGENCIES

1. Traders providing assessment services which fully satisfy the conditions and criteria suitable with assessment requirements shall have to perform assessment at the request of state agencies.

2. State agencies which request the assessment shall have to pay assessment remunerations to traders providing assessment services according to agreements between the two parties on the basis of market prices.

LEASE OF GOODS

Lease of goods means commercial activities whereby one party transfers the right to possess and use goods (referred to as lessor) to another party (referred to as lessee) for a certain duration to enjoy rentals.

RIGHTS AND OBLIGATIONS OF LESSORS

Unless otherwise agreed, lessors shall have the following rights and obligations:

1. To deliver leased goods to lessees as agreed upon in lease contracts;

2. To ensure that the right of lessees to possess and use leased goods is not disputed by a concerned third party in the lease duration;

3. To ensure that leased goods are suitable to the use purposes of lessees as agreed upon by the parties;

4. To maintain and repair leased goods within a reasonable duration. Where the maintenance and repair of leased goods cause harms to the use of such goods by lessees, lessors shall have to reduce rent rates or prolong lease duration corresponding to the time of maintenance and repair;

5. To receive rentals according to agreements or provisions of law;

6. To take back leased goods upon the expiration of the lease duration.

RIGHTS AND OBLIGATIONS OF LESSEES

Unless otherwise agreed, lessees shall have the following rights and obligations:

1. To possess and use leased goods according to lease contracts and the provisions of law. Where there is no specific agreement on the manner in which leased goods should be used, such leased goods shall be used in a manner appropriate to their nature;

2. To maintain and preserve leased goods in the lease duration and return such goods to lessors upon the expiration of the lease duration;

3. To request lessors to perform the maintenance and repair of goods. If lessors fail to perform such obligation within a reasonable period of time, lessees may perform the maintenance and repair of leased goods and lessors shall bear all reasonable expenses for such maintenance and repair;

4. To pay rentals as agreed or according to the provisions of law;

5. Not to sell or sub-lease the leased goods.

REPAIR OR ALTERATION OF ORIGINAL STATUS OF LEASED GOODS

1. Lessees must not repair or alter the original status of leased goods if not so consented by lessors.

2. Where lessees perform the repair or alter the original status of the leased goods without lessors' consents, lessors shall have the right to request lessees to restore the original status of the leased goods or claim damages.

LIABILITY FOR LOSS OCCURRING IN THE LEASE DURATION

1. Unless otherwise agreed, lessors shall bear loss of leased goods occurring in the lease duration if lessees are not at fault in causing such loss.

2. Lessors shall have to repair leased goods within a reasonable duration to ensure the achievement of use purposes of lessees.

PASS OF RISKS INCURRED TO LEASED GOODS

Where the parties agree on the pass of risk to the lessee but the point of time of passing risks is not determined, that point of time shall be determined as follows:

1. In cases where the lease contract involves the transportation of goods:

a/ If the contract does not require the leased goods to be delivered at a designated place, risks shall be passed to the lessee when the leased goods are delivered to the first carrier;

b/ If the contract requires the leased goods to be delivered at a designated place, risks shall be passed to the lessee or the person authorized by the lessee to receive the goods at such place;

2. In cases where the leased goods are received by a bailee other than a carrier for delivery, risks shall be passed to the lessee as soon as the bailee acknowledge the lessee's right to possess the leased goods;

LEASED GOODS INAPPROPRIATE TO CONTRACTS

Where there is no specific agreement, goods shall be deemed inappropriate to contracts when such goods fall into one of the following cases:

1. They are suitable to common utility of goods of the same type;

2. They are not suitable to specific purposes which the lessee has informed the lessor or the lessor should have known at the time the contract was entered into;

3. Their quality is not the same as goods samples handed over by the lessor to the lessee.

REJECTION OF GOODS

1. The lessor shall give the lessee a reasonable time after the receipt of goods for inspection thereof.

2. The lessee may reject the goods in the following cases:

a/ The lessor does not give conditions and a reasonable time to the lessee for inspecting the goods;

b/ When inspecting the goods, the lessee discovers that the goods are inappropriate to the contract.

RECTIFICATION OR REPLACEMENT OF LEASED GOODS INAPPROPRIATE TO CONTRACTS

Where the lessee rejects leased goods inappropriate to the contract, if the time limit for delivery of goods has not yet expired, the lessor may promptly notify the lessee of the rectification or replacement of the goods and then perform such rectification or replacement of goods within the remaining duration.

ACCEPTANCE OF LEASED GOODS

1. The lessee shall be deemed having accepted the leased goods after being given a reasonable opportunity to inspect the leased goods and taking one of the following acts:

a/ Not rejecting the leased goods;

b/ Certifying the appropriateness of the leased goods to agreements in the contract;

c/ Confirming the acceptance of the goods despite their inappropriateness to agreements in the contract.

2. If the lessee discovers the inappropriateness of the leased goods to the contract after accepting such goods and such inappropriateness is detectable through a reasonable inspection before the acceptance, the lessee shall not be entitled to rely on such inappropriateness as an excuse for returning the goods.

WITHDRAWAL OF ACCEPTANCE

1. Lessees may withdraw their acceptance of part or whole of the leased goods if the inappropriateness of such leased goods may render them unable to achieve the objectives of the entry into of contracts and falls into one of the following cases:

a/ Lessors fail to make reasonable rectification;

b/ Lessees fail to detect the inappropriateness of the goods due to lessors' guarantee.

2. The withdrawal of acceptance must be made within a reasonable period of time, which must not exceed three months as from the date lessees accept the goods.

SUB-LEASE

1. Lessees shall be entitled to sub-lease goods only when they obtain consents of lessors. Lessees shall be responsible for sub-leased goods, unless they otherwise agree with lessors.

2. Where lessees sub-lease leased goods without consents of lessors, lessors may revoke lease contracts. Sub-lessees shall have to return the goods to lessors immediately.

BENEFITS ARISING IN THE LEASE DURATION

Unless otherwise agreed, all benefits arising from leased goods in the lease duration shall belong to lessees.

CHANGE OF OWNERSHIP IN THE LEASE DURATION

Any change of ownership over leased goods shall not affect the validity of lease contracts.

COMMERCIAL FRANCHISE

Commercial franchise means a commercial activity whereby franchisors permit and require franchisees to undertake by themselves to purchase or sell goods or provide services on the following conditions:

1. The purchase or sale of goods or provision of services shall be conducted in accordance with methods of business organization prescribed by franchisors and associated with the franchisors' trademarks, trade names, business knows-how, business slogans, business logos and advertisements.

2. Franchisors shall be entitled to supervise and assist franchisees in conducting their business activities.

COMMERCIAL FRANCHISE CONTRACTS

Commercial franchise contracts must be made in writing or in other forms of equivalent legal validity.

RIGHTS OF FRANCHISORS

Unless otherwise agreed, franchisors shall have the following rights:

1. To receive franchise sums.

2. To organize advertising for the commercial franchise system and the commercial franchise network.

3. To conduct periodical or extraordinary inspections of activities of franchisees in order to ensure the uniformity of the commercial franchise system and the stability of quality of goods and services.

OBLIGATIONS OF FRANCHISORS

Unless otherwise agreed, franchisors shall have the following obligations:

1. To supply documents guiding the commercial franchise system to franchisees;

2. To provide initial training and regular technical assistance to franchisees for managing the latter's activities in accordance with the commercial franchise system;

3. To design and arrange places of sale of goods or provision of services at the expenses of franchisees;

4. To guarantee the intellectual property rights over objects stated in franchise contracts;

5. To equally treat all franchisees in the commercial franchise system.

RIGHTS OF FRANCHISEES

Unless otherwise agreed, franchisees shall have the following rights:

1. To request franchisors to provide fully technical assistance related to the commercial franchise system;

2. To request franchisors to equally treat all franchisees in the commercial franchise system.

OBLIGATIONS OF FRANCHISEES

Unless otherwise agreed, franchisees shall have the following obligations:

1. To pay franchise sums and other amounts under commercial franchise contracts;

2. To invest adequate material facilities, financial sources and human resources to take over business rights and know-how transferred by franchisors;

3. To submit to the control, supervision and instruction by franchisors; to comply with all requirements set forth by franchisors on designing and arrangement of places of sale of goods or provision of services;

4. To keep secret the franchised business know-how even after the expiration or termination of commercial franchise contracts;

5. To stop using trademarks, trade names, business slogans, logos and other intellectual property rights (if any) or systems of franchisors upon the expiration or termination of commercial franchise contracts;

6. To manage their activities in accordance with the commercial franchise system;

7. Not to sub-franchise without permissions of franchisors.

TYPES OF COMMERCIAL REMEDIES

1. Specific performance of contracts.

2. Fines for breaches.

3. Forcible payment of damages.

4. Suspension of performance of contracts.

5. Stoppage of performance of contracts.

6. Cancellation of contracts.

APPLICATION OF COMMERCIAL REMEDIES AGAINST INSUBSTANTIAL BREACHES

Unless otherwise agreed, aggrieved parties are not entitled to apply the remedy of suspension of performance of contracts, stoppage of performance of contracts or cancellation of contracts against insubstantial breaches.

CASES OF EXEMPTION FROM LIABILITY FOR BREACHING ACTS

1. A party that breaches a contract shall be exempted from liability in the following cases:

a/ A case of liability exemption agreed upon by the parties occurs;

b/ A force majeure event occurs;

c/ A breach by one party is entirely attributable to the other party's fault;

d/ A breach is committed by one party as a result of the execution of a decision of a competent state management agency which the party cannot know, at the time the contract is entered into.

2. The contract-breaching party shall bear the burden of proof of cases of liability exemption.

NOTIFICATION AND CERTIFICATION OF CASES OF LIABILITY EXEMPTION

1. The party must promptly notify in writing the other party of cases of liability exemption and possible consequences thereof.

2. When a case of liability exemption no longer exists, the contract-breaching party must promptly notify such to the other party. The breaching party must pay damages if it fails to notify or notifies the other party not in a prompt manner.

3. Breaching parties are obliged to prove their cases of liability exemption to aggrieved parties.

EXTENSION OF TIME LIMIT FOR PERFORMANCE OF CONTRACTS, OR REFUSAL TO PERFORM CONTRACTS IN FORCE MAJEURE CIRCUMSTANCES

In a force majeure circumstance, the parties may agree to extend the time limit for performing their respective contractual obligations. If the parties do not agree or cannot agree upon such extension, the time limit for performing contractual obligations shall be extended for a period of time equal to the time length of such force majeure circumstance plus a reasonable period of time for remedying consequences, but not exceeding:

a/ Five months for goods or services for which the agreed time limit for their delivery or provision does not exceed twelve months from the date the contract is entered into;

b/ Eight months for goods or services for which the agreed time limit for their delivery or provision exceeds twelve months from the date the contract is entered into.

SPECIFIC PERFORMANCE OF CONTRACTS

1. Specific performance of a contract means a remedy whereby the aggrieved party requests the breaching party to properly perform the contract or apply other measures to cause the contract to be performed and the breaching party shall have to bear any costs incurred.

2. Where the breaching party fails to deliver goods in full or provide services in accordance with the contract, it shall have to deliver goods in full or provide services in accordance with the contract. Where the breaching party delivers goods or provides services of inferior quality, it shall have to rectify defects of the goods or shortcomings of the services or to deliver other goods as substitutes or provide services in accordance with the contract. The breaching party must not use money or goods or services of other types as substitutes unless so consented by the aggrieved party.

FINE LEVEL

The fine level for a breach of a contractual obligation or the aggregate fine level for more than one breach shall be agreed upon in the contract by the parties but must not exceed 8% of the value of the breached contractual obligation portion, except for cases specified in Article 266 of commercial law.

DAMAGES

1. Damages means a remedy whereby the breaching party pays compensation for the loss caused by a contract-breaching act to the aggrieved party.

2. The value of damages covers the value of the material and direct loss suffered by the aggrieved party due to the breach of the breaching party and the direct profit which the aggrieved party would have earned if such breach had not been committed.

GROUNDS FOR LIABILITY TO PAY DAMAGES

Liability to pay damages shall arise upon existence of all of the following elements:

1. Breach of the contract;

2. Material loss;

3. Act of breaching the contract is the direct cause of the loss.

BURDEN OF PROOF OF LOSS

The party claiming damages shall bear the burden of proof of the loss, the extent of the loss caused by the act of breach, and direct profit amount which the aggrieved party would have earned if the breach had not been committed.

OBLIGATIONS TO MITIGATE LOSS

The party claiming damages must apply appropriate measures to mitigate the loss caused by a contract breach, including the loss of direct profit which it would have earned. If the party claiming damages fails to do so, the breaching party may request a rebate of the value of damages to the extent of the loss that would have been mitigated.

RIGHT TO CLAIM INTEREST ON DELAYED PAYMENT

Where a contract-breaching party delays making payment for goods or payment of service charges and other reasonable fees, the aggrieved party may claim an interest on such delayed payment at the average interest rate applicable to overdue debts in the market at the time of payment for the delayed period, unless otherwise agreed or provided for by law.

RELATIONSHIP BETWEEN REMEDY OF FINES AND REMEDY OF DAMAGES

1. Where the parties do not agree upon fines for breaches, the aggrieved party shall only be entitled to claim damages, unless otherwise provided for by commercial law.

2. Where the parties agree upon fines for breaches, the aggrieved party shall be entitled to apply both remedies of fines and damages, unless otherwise provided for by commercial law.

SUSPENSION OF PERFORMANCE OF CONTRACTS

Suspension of performance of a contract means a remedy whereby a party temporarily ceases the performance of its contractual obligations in one of the following cases:

1. Upon commission of a breaching act which serves as a condition for the suspension of performance of the contract as agreed upon by the parties;

2. Upon a substantial breach of contractual obligations by a party.

LEGAL CONSEQUENCES OF SUSPENSION OF PERFORMANCE OF CONTRACTS

1. Contracts which are suspended from performance are still in full force and effective.

2. Aggrieved parties are entitled to claim damages according to the provisions of commercial law.

STOPPAGE OF PERFORMANCE OF CONTRACTS

Stoppage of performance of a contract means a remedy whereby a party terminates the performance of its contractual obligations in one of the following cases:

1. Upon commission of a breaching act which serves as a condition for stoppage of the performance of the contract as agreed upon by the parties;

2. Upon a substantial breach of contractual obligations by a party.

LEGAL CONSEQUENCES OF STOPPAGE OF PERFORMANCE OF CONTRACTS

1. Where a contract is stopped from performance, it shall be terminated from the date when one party receives the notice on stoppage. The parties shall not have to further perform their contractual obligations. A party that has performed its contractual obligations may request the other party to pay or perform its reciprocal obligations.

2. The aggrieved party may claim damages according to the provisions of commercial law.

CANCELLATION OF CONTRACTS

1. Cancellation of a contract includes cancellation of part of a contract or cancellation of the entire contract.

2. Cancellation of the entire contract means the complete annulment of the performance of all contractual obligations for the entire contract.

3. Cancellation of part of a contract means the annulment of the performance of some contractual obligations while other parts of the contract are still valid.

4. The remedy of cancellation of contracts shall be applied in the following cases:

a/ Upon commission of a breaching act which serves as a condition for the cancellation of the contract as agreed upon by the parties;

b/ Upon a substantial breach of contractual obligations by a party.

CANCELLATION OF CONTRACTS IN CASE OF DELIVERY OF GOODS OR PROVISION OF SERVICES IN INSTALLMENTS

1. Where there is an agreement on delivery of goods or provision of services in installments, if one party fails to perform its obligation for the delivery of goods or provision of services and such failure constitutes a substantial breach in that time of delivery of goods or provision of services, the other party shall have the right to declare the cancellation of the contract for such delivery of goods or provision of services.

2. Where the failure of a party to perform its obligation for a delivery of goods or a provision of services serves as the basis for the other party to conclude that a substantial breach of the contract shall happen in subsequent deliveries of goods or provisions of services, the aggrieved party shall have the right to declare the cancellation of the contract for subsequent deliveries of goods or provisions of services, provided that such party must exercise that right within a reasonable period of time.

3. Where a party has declared the cancellation of a contract for a single delivery of goods or provision of services, such party shall still have the right to declare the cancellation of the contract for a delivery of goods or provision of services that has been conducted or will be conducted subsequently if the interrelation between the deliveries of goods makes the delivered goods or provided services unable to be used for the purposes intended by the parties at the time they enter into the contract.

LEGAL CONSEQUENCES OF CANCELLATION OF CONTRACTS

1. The parties shall have the right to claim benefits brought about by their performance of their contractual obligations. Where both parties have indemnity obligations, their obligations must be performed concurrently. Where it is impossible to make the indemnity with benefits which one party has enjoyed, the obliged party must make the indemnity in cash.

2. Aggrieved parties are entitled to claim damages according to the provisions of commercial law.

NOTIFICATION OF SUSPENSION OF PERFORMANCE OF CONTRACTS, STOPPAGE OF PERFORMANCE OF CONTRACTS OR CANCELLATION OF CONTRACTS

A party that suspends the performance of a contract, stops the performance of a contract or cancels a contract must immediately notify the other party of such suspension, stoppage or cancellation. Where a failure to do so causes a loss to the other party, the party that suspends the performance of the contract, stops the performance of the contract or cancels the contract must pay damages.

RIGHT TO CLAIM DAMAGES WHEN OTHER REMEDIES HAVE BEEN APPLIED

A party shall not lose its right to claim damages for the loss caused by a contract breach by the other party when other remedies have been applied.

FORMS OF RESOLUTION OF DISPUTES

1. Negotiations between the parties.

2. Conciliation between the parties by a body, organization or individual selected by the parties to act as the conciliation mediator.

3. Resolution by the Arbitration or the Court.

Procedures for resolution of commercial disputes by arbitration or a court shall comply with procedures applicable to arbitrations or courts provided for by law.

ACTS OF VIOLATION OF COMMERCIAL LAW

Acts of violation of commercial law include:

a/ Violating provisions on business registration; business licenses of traders; establishment and operation of representative offices and branches of traders;

b/ Violating provisions on domestically traded goods and services, and exported or imported goods and services; temporary import for re-export, temporary export for re-import; transfer through border-gates; transit;

c/ Violating provisions on taxes, invoices, documents, accounting books and reports;

d/ Violating provisions on prices of goods and services;

e/ Violating provisions on labeling of domestically circulated goods and exports and imports;

f/ Smuggling, trading in goods illegally imported, counterfeit goods or raw materials and materials for production of counterfeit goods, or conducting illegal business;

g/ Violating provisions on quality of domestically traded goods and services, and exported or imported goods and services;

h/ Defrauding and deceiving customers in the purchase and sale of goods or the provision of services;

i/ Violating provisions on protection of interests of customers;

j/ Violating provisions on intellectual property rights to domestically traded goods and services; and exported or imported goods and services;

k/ Violating provisions on origin of goods;

l/ Other violations in commercial activities according to the provisions of law.

FORMS OF HANDLING OF VIOLATIONS OF COMMERCIAL LAW

1. Depending on the nature, seriousness and consequences of violations, violating organizations and individuals shall be handled in one of the following forms:

a/ Sanctions according to the provisions of law on handling of administrative violations;

b/ Where an act of violation involves all elements constituting a crime, the violator shall be examined for penal liability according to the provisions of law.

2. Where an act of violation causes harm to the interests of the State or legitimate rights and interests of organizations and/or individuals, compensation must be paid according to the provisions of law.

SANCTIONING OF ADMINISTRATIVE VIOLATIONS IN COMMERCIAL ACTIVITIES

The Government shall specify the sanctioning of administrative violations in commercial activities.

CONCLUSION

Thank you again for downloading this book on *"COMMERCIAL LAW: Essential Legal Terms Explained You Need to Know About Law on Commerce!"* and reading all the way to the end. I'm extremely grateful.

If you know of anyone else who may benefit from the informative legal words presented in this book, please help me inform them of this book. I would greatly appreciate it.

Finally, if you enjoyed this book and feel that it has added value to your study or career in any way, please take a couple of minutes to share your thoughts and post a REVIEW on Amazon. Your feedback will help me to continue to write the kind of Kindle books that helps you get results. Furthermore, if you write a simple REVIEW with positive words for this book on Amazon, you can help hundreds or perhaps thousands of other readers who may want to enhance their legal vocabulary have a chance getting what they need. Like you, they worked hard for every penny they spend on books. With the information and recommendation you provide, they would be more likely to take action right away. We really look forward to reading your review.

Thanks again for your support and good luck!

If you enjoy my book, please write a POSITIVE REVIEW on amazon.

-- Dr. Peter Johnson --

Check Out Other Books

Go here to check out other related books that might interest you:

Legal Terminology And Phrases: Essential Legal Terms Explained You Need To Know About Crimes, Penalty And Criminal Procedure

http://www.amazon.com/dp/B01L5EB54Y

LAW ON INTELLECTUAL PROPERTY: Essential Legal Terms Explained You Need To Know About Trademarks, Copyrights, Patents, and Trade Secrets!

https://www.amazon.com/dp/B07PFP3MDY

COMPANY LAW: Mastering Essential Legal Terms Explained About Limited Liability Companies, Joint-Stock Companies, Partnership, Private Enterprises, And Groups of Companies!

https://www.amazon.com/dp/B07P2PRVMJ

TAX LAW: Essential Legal Terms Explained You Need To Know About Types of Tax Law!

https://www.amazon.com/dp/B07PH1L3RS

LAW ON LAWYERS: Essential Legal Terms Explained You Need To Know About Law on Lawyers!

https://www.amazon.com/dp/B07PH9SCBN

INVESTMENT LAW: Essential Legal Terms Explained You Need To Know About Law On Investment!

https://www.amazon.com/dp/B07P79D925

LABOR LAW: Essential Legal Terms Explained You Need To Know About Law On Labor!

https://www.amazon.com/dp/B07PFD2CML

CIVIL LAW: Mastering Essential Legal Terms Explained About Civil Rights, Guardianship, Civil Transactions, Civil Obligations, Civil Liability, Civil Contracts And Civil Procedure!

https://www.amazon.com/dp/B07P5GS8LD

Legal Vocabulary In Use: Master 600+ Essential Legal Terms And Phrases Explained In 10 Minutes A Day

http://www.amazon.com/dp/B01L0FKXPU

Civil Law Vocabulary In Use: Master 350+ Essential Civil Law Terms And Phrases Explained With Examples In 10 Minutes A Day.

https://www.amazon.com/dp/B0781TQWGV

Criminal Law Vocabulary In Use: Master 400+ Essential Criminal Law Terms And Phrases Explained With Examples In 10 Minutes A Day.

https://www.amazon.com/dp/B078KLR51Z

Administrative And Tax Law In Use : Master 300+ Administrative And Tax Law Terms And Phrases Explained With Examples In 10 Minutes A Day.

https://www.amazon.com/dp/B07JMD546J

www.ingramcontent.com/pod-product-compliance
Lightning Source LLC
Chambersburg PA
CBHW021812170526
45157CB00007B/2561